DISAPPEARING ACTS

Green Tree Frogs
Colorful Hiders

by Natalie Lunis

Consultant: Dr. Kenneth L. Krysko
Senior Biological Scientist, Division of Herpetology
Florida Museum of Natural History, University of Florida

BEARPORT
PUBLISHING

NEW YORK, NEW YORK

Credits

Cover, © David M. Schleser/Nature's Images/Photo Researchers, Inc. and Elenathewise/Fotolia; TOC, © MediaMagnet/Wileys/SuperStock; 4-5, © David M. Schleser/Nature's Images/Photo Researchers, Inc.; 6, © Bob F/Alamy; 7, © Graeme Teague Photography; 9, © Hal Horwitz/Corbis; 11, © fotoIE/iStockphoto; 12, © Jon R. Katze; 13, © Clive Varlack/Clivevbugs; 14, © Stephen Dalton/Animals Animals Enterprises; 15, © Joe McDonald/Corbis; 16, © McDonald Wildlife Photography/Animals Animals Enterprises; 17, © John P. Clare/FrogForum.net; 19, © Dirk J. Stevenson; 20, © Professor R. Wayne Van Devender; 21, © Stephen Dalton/Minden Pictures; 22L, © Scott W. Smith/Animals Animals Enterprises; 22C, © Alan Weaver Wildlife Photos; 22R, © Juniors Bildarchiv/Alamy; 23TL, © David M. Schleser/Nature's Images/Photo Researchers, Inc.; 23TR, © Clive Varlack/Clivevbugs; 23CL, © Nykonchuk Oleksii/Shutterstock; 23CR, © Galushko Sergey/Shutterstock; 23BL, © Dirk J. Stevenson; 23BR, © Heath Doman/iStockphoto.

Publisher: Kenn Goin
Editorial Director: Adam Siegel
Creative Director: Spencer Brinker
Design: Kim Jones
Photo Researcher: Jennifer Bright

Library of Congress Cataloging-in-Publication Data

Lunis, Natalie.
  Green tree frogs : colorful hiders / by Natalie Lunis.
     p. cm. — (Disappearing Acts)
  Includes bibliographical references and index.
  ISBN-13: 978-1-936087-44-0 (library binding)
  ISBN-10: 1-936087-44-8 (library binding)
  1. Green treefrog—Juvenile literature. 2. Camouflage (Biology)—Juvenile literature. I. Title.
  QL668.E24L86 2010
  597.87'82—dc22

                              2009038595

For more information, write to Bearport Publishing Company, Inc., 101 Fifth Avenue, Suite 6R, New York, New York 10003. Printed in the United States of America in North Mankato, Minnesota.

112009
090309CGC

10 9 8 7 6 5 4 3 2 1

Contents

Leafy Hideouts

The **wetlands** of Florida and other southeastern states stay warm and green most of the year.

They are home to many kinds of trees and plants.

Don't be tricked by their bright green leaves, however.

There may be more to them than meets the eye.

Some of them are hiding places for little green tree frogs!

The green tree frog's bright green skin acts as **camouflage**, blending in almost perfectly with green leaves.

Daytime Dozers

Green tree frogs sleep during the day.

They tuck in their legs and hang on to a green leaf or stem.

As they doze all day, they stay very still.

They also stay safe.

It's not easy for hungry enemies such as birds and snakes to see them.

In spite of their name, green tree frogs don't live only in trees. They spend time on many kinds of plants that grow in or near water, including bushes, tall grasses, and water lilies.

Stand-out Stripes

There are about 1,200 kinds of tree frogs.

The green tree frog—which is also known as the American green tree frog—has a white stripe running along each side of its bright green body.

Many people call it a racing stripe.

It helps them tell the green tree frog apart from other kinds of tree frogs.

Where Green Tree Frogs Live

UNITED STATES

Pacific Ocean

Atlantic Ocean

N
W E
S

☐ Green tree frogs

American green tree frogs are found in most of the southeastern United States. They also live as far north as Delaware and as far west as Texas.

racing stripe

Nighttime Hunters

When nighttime comes, green tree frogs wake up and start to move around.

They climb up trees and plants or walk along the ground to search for food.

Mosquitoes, flies, crickets, and moths are some of the **insects** that they hunt.

As soon as a frog comes close enough to one of these tasty creatures, it flicks out its long, sticky tongue.

Zap—the insect is caught!

Making House Calls

Green tree frogs often show up at people's houses.

Why?

They follow the many insects that are attracted to lights in windows and on porches.

Often the frogs stay around, sleeping on the leaves of nearby trees and plants.

At night they sometimes climb up windows and sliding glass doors as they hunt for food.

Like all tree frogs, green tree frogs have sticky pads at the ends of their toes. These **toe pads** help them climb up tree trunks, plant stems, and tall leaves, as well as glass windows and doors.

toe pads

13

Little but Loud

Quonk, quonk, quonk!

During spring and summer, the calls of green tree frogs fill the night air.

Some people say the calls sound like clinking cowbells.

Others say they sound like honking horns.

Whatever they sound most like, the calls come only from males.

They have one clear purpose—to attract a female mate.

green tree frog calling

vocal sac

As a male green tree frog calls, a pocket of skin on its throat, called a vocal sac, fills up with air.

Eggs in the Water

Male green tree frogs send out their calls from a spot that is near water.

That way, when a female comes to him in order to mate, she won't have to go far to lay her eggs.

Like all frogs, green tree frogs lay their eggs in ponds and other watery places.

Female green tree frogs lay up to 400 eggs at a time. Usually they attach them in groups on the roots of plants that are floating in water.

male green tree frog calling for a mate

Tiny Tadpoles

After about five days, the eggs hatch.

The baby green tree frogs that come out are called **tadpoles**.

They do not look like frogs at all.

Instead, they look more like fish, since they have a long tail and no legs.

They breathe underwater using body parts called gills and swim around looking for food.

At first a tadpole's gills are on the outside of its body. After about three weeks the outside gills disappear, and new gills form inside the tadpole's body.

Big Changes

Young tree frogs stay in the water only for the early part of their lives.

About ten weeks after hatching, their bodies begin to change in ways that allow them to live on land.

The tadpoles start growing front and back legs.

Body parts for breathing air, called lungs, take the place of their gills.

Soon the little creatures will be ready to leave the water.

They will start their lives as tree frogs, hunting insects at night and hiding on leaves during the day as they sleep.

legs

As a tadpole grows into a frog, its tail gets shorter and shorter until it finally disappears completely.

More Disappearing Acts

Green tree frogs aren't the only creatures that hide by disappearing among trees and plants. Here are three more animals that are camouflaged to blend in with leaves, stems, and bark.

Green Anole

Green Swallowtail Butterfly

Peppered Moth

Glossary

camouflage
(KAM-uh-flahzh)
colors and markings
on an animal's body
that help it blend in
with its surroundings

toe pads
(TOH PADZ) round,
sticky parts at the
ends of a tree frog's
feet

insects (IN-sekts)
small animals that have
six legs, three body
parts, two antennas,
and a hard covering
called an exoskeleton

wetlands
(WET-*landz*)
swampy areas near
lakes and rivers

tadpoles
(TAD-pohlz) baby frogs
that live in water

Index

Read More

Frost, Helen. *Tree Frogs*. Mankato, MN: Pebble Books (2002).

Netherton, John. *Red-Eyed Tree Frogs*. Minneapolis, MN: Lerner (2001).

Weir, Diana Loiewski. *Tree Frogs*. Mankato, MN: Creative Education (2000).

Learn More Online

To learn more about green tree frogs, visit
www.bearportpublishing.com/DisappearingActs

About the Author

Natalie Lunis has written many science and nature books for children. She hides out among the leaves and trees in the Hudson River Valley, just north of New York City.